PREHISTORIC ANIMALS

ICE AGE BEASTS

MICHAEL JAY

Raintree

Chicago, Illinois

For information about the publisher:
Raintree, 100 N. LaSalle, Suite 1200, Chicago, IL 60602
Customer Service 888-363-4266
Visit our website at www.raintreelibrary.com

Printed in China and bound in the United States.
07 06 05 04 03
10 9 8 7 6 5 4 3 2 1

Library of Congress Cataloging-in-Publication Data:

Jay, Michael, 1956-
  Ice Age beasts / Michael Jay.
    p. cm. -- (Prehistoric animals)
Includes bibliographical references and index.
Contents: Freezer planet -- Before the ice age -- Icy blanket -- Hairy
giant -- Beast with horns -- Saber tooth! -- Forest beasts -- Horns and
teeth -- Southern giants -- Life down under -- A warmer world -- Ice age words -- Ice age facts -- Ice age beasts summary -- Ice age beasts on the web.

  ISBN 1-4109-0008-8 (lib. bdg.)

  1. Animals, Fossil--Juvenile literature. 2. Paleontology--Pleistocene. 3. Glacial epoch. [1. Mammals, Fossil. 2.Prehistoric animals. 3. Paleontology--Pleistocene. 4. Glacial epoch.]
I. Title. II. Series: Jay, Michael, 1956- Prehistoric animals.
  QE741.2.J39 2004
  560'.1792--dc21

                              2003003647

Acknowledgments
The publishers would like to thank the following for permission to reproduce photographs:
pp. 1, 16 (tl), 26 (tl) Science Photo Library; pp. 2, 8 (bl), 14, 20 (bl), 23 (t), 24 (b), 28 Natural History Museum; p. 3 Gavin Page; pp. 4 (b), 5 (tr), 6, 7 (t), 8 (tl), 9, 10, 11, 12, 13, 18, 19 (br), 20 (tl), 22, 23 (br), 24 (tl), 27 (br), 29, 30, 32 Alpha Archive; pp. 4 (tl), 7 (b), 15 Peter Bull Artists; p. 20 (tl) Bernard Long; p. 25 Corbis Images; all other illustrations John Sibbick.

Every effort has been made to contact copyright holders of any material reproduced in this book. Any omissions will be rectified in subsequent printings if notice is given to the publishers.

▲ The woolly rhinoceros, *Coelodonta*, lived in the snows bordering the great glaciers of Earth's northern lands.

CONTENTS

LOOK FOR THE MAMMOTH BOX

Look for the mammoth logo in boxes like this.
Here you will find extra facts, stories, and other
interesting information.

FREEZER PLANET

From time to time, Earth has gone through very cold periods known as ice ages. During each ice age, large parts of the world have been covered in vast sheets of ice.

▲ Woolly rhinoceroses once roamed across snowy plains in Asia.

There have been many ice ages in Earth's history. The most severe of them turned much of the planet into a chilly snowball for millions of years.

The most recent ice ages lasted from about 1.6 million years ago to 10,000 years ago. During this time, called the Pleistocene, the ice came and went many times and the world's temperature became warmer or colder. In the cold spells, much of the northern half of the planet was frozen under layers of ice that were hundreds of feet deep.

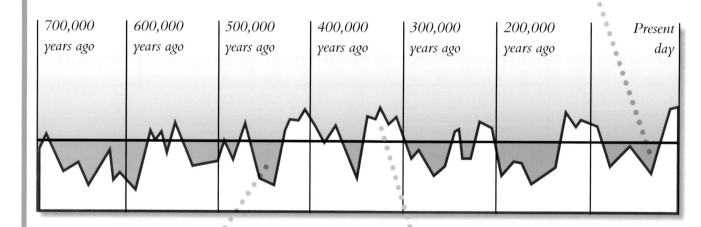

coldest part of last ice age, 18,000–20,000 years ago

700,000 years ago | 600,000 years ago | 500,000 years ago | 400,000 years ago | 300,000 years ago | 200,000 years ago | *Present day*

cold periods　　*warm periods*

▲ In the last 700,000 years, there have been eight ice ages when the climate dipped into cold spells.

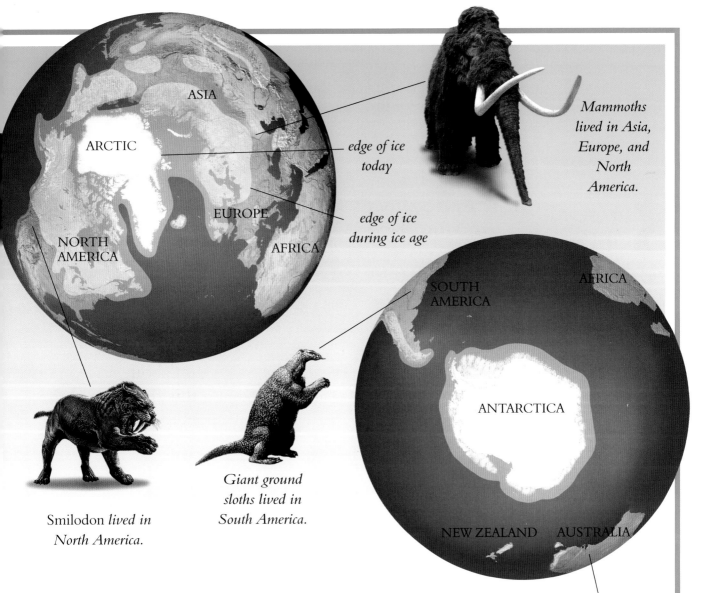

ASIA

ARCTIC

NORTH
AMERICA

EUROPE

AFRICA

*edge of ice
today*

*edge of ice
during ice age*

*Mammoths
lived in Asia,
Europe, and
North
America.*

SOUTH
AMERICA

AFRICA

ANTARCTICA

NEW ZEALAND   AUSTRALIA

Smilodon *lived in
North America.*

*Giant ground
sloths lived in
South America.*

*Marsupial lions
lived in Australia.*

▲ During the Pleistocene ice ages, thick sheets of ice covered
the areas shown on these globes. Few animals actually lived
on the ice, where there was little or no food to be found.

During the coldest parts of the Pleistocene ice ages, almost
one-third of Earth's land area was covered with ice. Some of
the animals that lived then were familiar-looking creatures,
such as wolves and bears. But others were strange-looking
beasts, unlike any animals living today.

Ice still covers large areas around the North and South
Poles, and high mountains. We live in a warmer time, but
there may be another ice age in the far future.

ICY BLANKET

As temperatures dropped, ice sheets advanced to places that had been warmer, grinding their way over the landscape at up to 3 feet (1 meter) per day.

glacier more than 1 mi (1.6 km) thick

During the Pleistocene ice ages, huge glaciers and vast ice sheets covered much of North America, Europe, and Asia. They covered Antarctica completely. The ice could be very thick. Wide areas were covered with layers of packed ice more than 1 mile (1.6 kilometers) deep.

Animals in the cold zones had a daily battle to survive. Many plants were buried in snow, making it difficult for plant-eating animals to find food. Many animals grew thick, shaggy coats for warmth in the freezing conditions.

◀ The world's tallest office buildings are presently the Petronas Towers in Malaysia. But as big as they are, these 1,482-ft (452-m) high structures are tiny compared to many ice age glaciers.

Petronas Towers

During ice age summers, temperatures became a little warmer and some ice melted from the glaciers. Water from the melting ice became chilly streams that gushed across the land. The flowing water helped plants grow again, and animals could find more to eat.

WHAT IS A GLACIER?

A glacier is a river of ice that moves slowly downhill, grinding away anything that stands in the way. Soil, rocks, and entire landscapes can be crushed by the moving ice. The top of a glacier can be covered in fresh snow, but as the snow builds up, its weight crushes the layers below to form a solid mass of heavy ice.

There are many glaciers today, but they are formed only near the poles and in high mountain areas. The one pictured here is in the Canadian Rocky Mountains.

▼ This is how an ice age glacier might have looked at its foot, or lowest point. The ice dumped a constant supply of water, rocks, and gravel.

running streams and waterfalls caused by melting ice

Mammoths eating grass and other vegetation

CAVE CREATURES

Many animals escaped the icy chill by moving to warmer lands. Other animals used caves as shelter during the long, cold winters.

▲ A glacier scraped out this rugged cliff at Creswell Crags in Great Britain. The caves were used by many animals over the years.

One of the cave-dwelling animals was the 7 foot (2 meter) cave bear, *Ursus spelaeus.* This big bear lived across much of Europe during the Pleistocene, escaping the deep freeze by sleeping through the winter in caves. Researchers have found a large cave in Austria that is littered with the bones of dead bears. It seems that many bears shared the cave, and a few died each winter. Over thousands of years the cave turned into a huge bear graveyard.

The cave lion *Panthera leo spelaea* was another animal that sheltered in caves. It grew up to about 11.5 feet (3.5 meters) long, and lived in Europe as far north as Denmark, until about 2,000 years ago.

◄ Cave bears did not survive to the present day. They were common in Europe throughout the Pleistocene ice ages.

Hyenas were hunting animals that used caves as dens during the last ice age. Caves provided safe shelter for pups, and freshly killed animals could be dragged to the safety of the cave to eat. Remains show that ice age hyenas hunted mostly bison, but also horses and reindeer.

▲ Until about 20,000 years ago, hyenas lived in much of Europe. They hunted in packs and also ate scraps left by other predators. Today hyenas live only in Africa.

 EARLY HUMAN HUNTERS

Scientists think that early humans showed up on Earth about 1 million years ago, and survived many ice age periods. Humans often used caves as homes and hunted many of the animals shown in this book. Some hunters decorated the walls of their caves with hunting scenes that show mammoths and bison. People also learned to store meat rather than have to eat a whole carcass in one sitting. In summer, the meat was dried, and in winter, it was left to freeze in the snow. The frozen meat could be cooked later over a roaring fire.

HAIRY GIANT

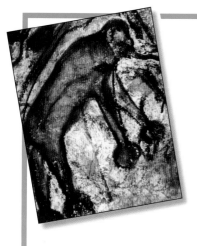

The mammoth is probably the best-known ice age animal. This huge beast had a thick, hairy coat that protected it from the bitter cold.

▲ Early humans often decorated their caves with paintings of mammoths. Most of the paintings have been found in caves in France and Spain. The art is thought to be about 30,000 years old.

Mammoths lived across much of North America, Europe, and Asia. Adults could grow to more than 9 feet (3 meters) tall. They spent their lives in herds, wandering through woods and grasslands, eating the plants that grew there.

Not all mammoths lived in snowy areas. For example, the imperial mammoth lived farther south and grew to about 13 feet (4 meters) high.

The earliest mammoths appeared about 2 million years ago. But a few may have survived to much more recent times. Some remains found on a chilly Siberian island may be only about 4,000 years old.

◄ Apart from humans, wolves were the only enemy that mammoths faced. A pack of hungry wolves could chase and eventually bring down a sick or injured mammoth.

*domed head and
shoulder hump*

▶ Woolly mammoths
had shaggy hair that
could grow nearly
3 ft (1 m) long. The
mammoth used its
trunk for feeling
and grasping things,
similar to the way
we use our hands.

CURVING TUSKS

Mammoths had two huge, curving tusks that sometimes
grew so long that they crossed over each other. Males
used their tusks at mating time to fight one another over
females. Tusks were also useful for sweeping aside snow
to get at buried food.

BODY IN THE ICE

6-ft (2-m) long trunk

The biggest mammoths weighed up to 10 tons.

Mammoths ate up to 496 lbs (225 kg) of food a day, mostly grass.

▲ Mammoths had a layer of fat up to 4 in (10 cm) thick under their skin.

We know more about ice age beasts than we do about earlier creatures such as the dinosaurs. This is because remains of their bodies have been found frozen in ice.

SIBERIA

young mammoth called Dima found here

Although we do not live in an ice age now, northern Siberia remains very cold, and much of the land stays frozen all year round to a depth of 1,650 feet (500 meters). Even in summer, only the top few feet thaw out.

It was in Siberia that a young male mammoth was found by miners digging for gold in 1977. The miners were using bulldozers to clear away frozen soil, and this is how the mammoth was discovered. When it died the animal was only about nine months old. One autumn day it had slipped and drowned in a deep mud pool. When winter came, the body was frozen solid.

▲ The young mammoth found in Siberia was named Dima after a nearby stream.

WHAT'S IN A NAME?

The word "mammoth" comes from the very old Siberian word *mammot,* meaning "earth burrower." Instead of being an animal from the past, the mammoth was thought to be a giant underground beast, like a huge mole. People believed that when an earth burrower came to the surface, it died in the open air. This explained why only remains were found, instead of living animals.

The mammoth, named Dima, was less than 3 feet (1 meter) high and still had its first set of teeth, the first of six sets that mammoths grew during their lives.

Dima died about 40,000 years ago, but scientists managed to find traces of the last meal, grass, in his stomach. Other ice age beasts have been dug up, but Dima's is the most complete body that has been found.

HORNED BEASTS

There were several kinds of ice age rhinoceros. The biggest of them weighed nearly 4 tons and had a huge horn growing out of its forehead.

The 19-foot (6-meter) long *Elasmotherium* lived in Europe and Asia during the Pleistocene, until about 10,000 years ago.

The *Elasmotherium*'s horn was made of the same hard material as fingernails, and most experts think it was huge, growing up to 6 feet (2 meters) long.

▲ Like all rhinos, the *Elasmotherium* was a plant-eater, surviving on a mixture of grasses, twigs, shoots, and leaves.

The woolly rhino, *Coelodonta,* was smaller than the *Elasmotherium* and had a thick, hairy coat for warmth with two large, curving horns on its head.

Today's rhinoceros is known for its short sight and for being easily startled. The woolly rhino was probably similar. In a fight, its huge front horn would have made a good weapon to sweep aside other animals. The horn could also have been used to shovel snow from side to side, so the plant-eating woolly rhino could reach grass growing under the snow.

ARE THEY CLAWS OR HORNS?

Many remains of woolly rhinos have been found, especially in northern Russia, where their bodies were frozen solid in the icy soil of Siberia. Remains were first found in the 1800s, but at first researchers thought the strange, curved horn was the claw of a giant prehistoric bird. More recent discoveries include some 30,000-year-old rhino skeletons dug up in a British quarry in 2002. The skeletons were found with some ice age plants that looked as if they had been buried for only a few weeks! Today there are five kinds of rhinos: two in Africa and three in Asia. The Sumatran rhino is the woolly rhino's closest surviving relative.

big hump over the shoulders

▼ An adult woolly rhino weighed more than 2 tons. These animals lived in many parts of Europe and Asia, but no remains have been found in North America.

front horn curved like a sword blade

SABER TOOTH

Saber-toothed cats were named after their huge, front teeth shaped like a curved sword, called a saber. There were several different kinds of these ferocious animals.

▶ Many prehistoric animals were preserved after they fell into the sticky La Brea tar pits in California. Here a *Smilodon* feasts on a dead body before it sinks into the tar.

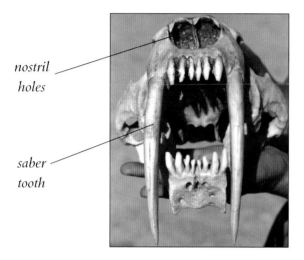

nostril holes

saber tooth

◀ *Smilodon* had jaws that opened very wide to allow its huge teeth to strike at prey.

Saber-toothed cats lived from more than 5 million years ago to about 10,000 years ago. Various kinds lived in North and South America, Africa, Europe, and Asia. One of the biggest was the *Smilodon*. It grew to nearly 9 feet (3 meters), larger than today's tiger. *Smilodon* had powerful front legs and shoulders, which allowed it to wrestle animals to the ground easily.

Saber-toothed cats had very sharp teeth, but they chipped easily if the cat bit too hard on bone. The teeth were brittle, too, and could snap if prey twisted strongly. So a *Smilodon* aimed to kill with one swift bite to the soft parts of its prey's neck. The cat's jaws opened very wide to allow its 10-inch (25 centimeter) long fangs a quick, deep, slicing thrust.

FIGHTING FOR SURVIVAL

Smilodon was larger than a present-day tiger and was one of the fiercest prehistoric hunting animals. But these big cats did not have it all that easy—many prey animals fought back strongly. Many *Smilodon* remains show minor injuries (such as broken teeth), while other remains show more serious injuries, including broken hip bones and jaws.

Smilodon

HUGE ANTLERS

The *Megaloceros* was a large Pleistocene deer that lived through the ice ages, from about 400,000 years ago until less than 10,000 years ago.

▲ The first antlered deer was the *Dicrocerus* of 7 million years ago.

The male *Megaloceros* had the biggest antlers of any deer that has ever lived. A full-grown adult male was nearly 9 feet (3 meters) tall, and its antlers could grow to more than 9 feet (3 meters) across.

◄ Only the male *Megaloceros* had huge antlers. These large deer lived in most of Europe and parts of Central Asia.

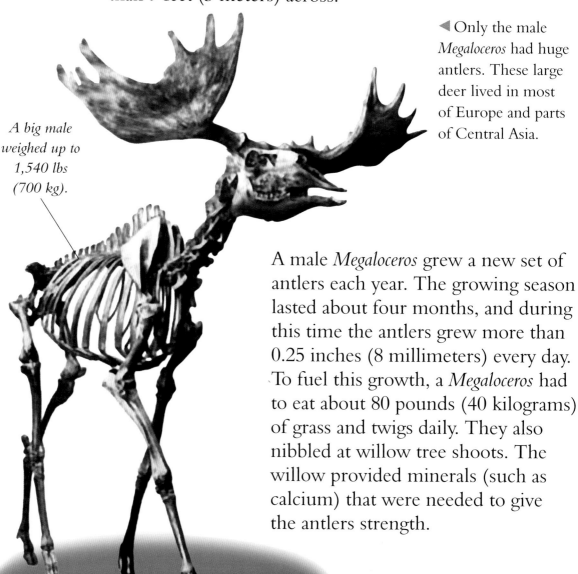

A big male weighed up to 1,540 lbs (700 kg).

A male *Megaloceros* grew a new set of antlers each year. The growing season lasted about four months, and during this time the antlers grew more than 0.25 inches (8 millimeters) every day. To fuel this growth, a *Megaloceros* had to eat about 80 pounds (40 kilograms) of grass and twigs daily. They also nibbled at willow tree shoots. The willow provided minerals (such as calcium) that were needed to give the antlers strength.

12 ft (3.6 m)

5.5 ft (1.7 m)

◀ Scientists have found remains of *Megaloceros* that are only 9,200 years old. These recent survivors may have been hunted by early human tribes.

A full set of tough antlers was needed in late August. This time of year was when the male *Megaloceros* used its antlers for display and to fight other males to see which animal could mate with the female deer.

Strength was needed for the many fights that followed. These were very tiring, even for a big stag with antlers that weighed up to 80 pounds (40 kilograms).

After mating, males and females lived apart. Soon the huge antlers fell off, to be replaced by a new set that started growing the following spring.

MEGA BEAVER

In North America, a giant beaver called the *Castoroides* lived in the lakes and forests. An adult *Castoroides* had a scaly tail and 6-in (15-cm) long cutting teeth. It grew to 8 ft (2.5 m) long and weighed about 400 lbs (200 kg), seven times more than a beaver of today.

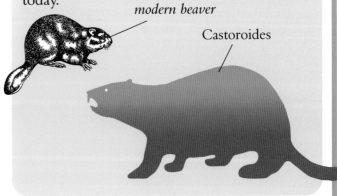

modern beaver

Castoroides

SOUTHERN GIANTS

Macrauchenia grew over 6 ft tall (2 m) at the shoulder.

▲ Huge herds of *Macrauchenia* lived on grassy plains until 10,000 years ago.

While much of the north was frozen during the Pleistocene, most of South America was much warmer. It had many of its own animal species.

South America was once an island. It joined with North America only about 3 to 4 million years ago. Until then South America's animals had developed separately and there were many strange beasts that lived nowhere else.

For example, the camel-sized *Macrauchenia* had a short trunk, like that of a modern tapir. The *Megatherium* was a huge ground sloth that weighed up to 3 tons.

◄ Giant ground sloths used their tails as a useful prop when plucking leaves from trees. The *Megatherium* was the biggest sloth, growing up to 19 ft (6 m) long. It was the biggest sloth ever known. Today's sloths that hang from the branches of trees are its distant relatives.

Glyptodonts were South America's living tanks—they had thick armor to protect them. Glyptodonts came in various sizes, but the biggest was the *Doedicurus,* which grew up to 9 feet (3 meters) long and weighed more than a ton. It was the ancestor of the modern armadillo, a much smaller animal.

For a predator, killing a glyptodont was quite a challenge. The body was covered in a shell of six-sided scales (called scutes), and some kinds had an armored tail that ended in a 80-pound (40-kilogram) spiked ball. One hit from this and any soft-skinned animal would have been injured or killed.

▲ Predators attack a glyptodont. They stand a good chance of bringing it down by attacking in a team rather than working alone.

WALKING TO A NEW WORLD

It seems odd to think that continents move, but they do, although very slowly.. North and South America eventually joined together at a narrow neck of land called the Isthmus of Panama. After this happened, animals from both sides could walk to new lands. North American animals that moved south included mice, squirrels, bears, and wolves. Animals such as opossums, sloths, and armadillos went north. Not all these creatures survived in their new homes—giant ground sloths died out in North America a few thousand years ago. But the armadillo is still spreading across Texas and other southern U.S. states.

Isthmus of Panama

LIFE DOWN UNDER

▲ The *Thylacoleo* lion weighed up to about 286 lbs (130 kg). The *Diprotodon* weighed more than 2 tons.

Australia and New Zealand were mostly untouched by the great ice sheets of the Pleistocene. Giant wombats lived in Australia and huge birds lived in New Zealand.

The mammals of Pleistocene Australia were all marsupials. These are animals that carry and feed their young in a pouch. The biggest marsupial of all was the *Diprotodon,* a large wombat the size of a modern hippopotamus. *Diprotodon* was a plant-eater. Remains of these creatures have been found in deep mud, where they were trapped when trying to reach vegetation.

The *Thylacoleo* was a giant marsupial lion with deadly front teeth and claws that could snap in and out of its paws. The first complete skeleton was found in a cave in western Australia in 2002. The bones are thought to have been there for about 1.5 million years.

ALIVE OR EXTINCT?

Until a few thousand years ago, the doglike *Thylacinus* was common in Australia. *Thylacinus* could run steadily over long distances, chasing prey until it was exhausted and could be killed easily. The last-known Tasmanian wolf, a later and smaller version of *Thylacinus,* died in a zoo in 1936. But there are sometimes reports of odd survivors living in remote areas.

stripes only on rear half of body

The 440 lb (200 kg) *Procoptodon* could hop along at more than 31 mph (50 km/h).

The biggest marsupial today is the red kangaroo. It grows to about 5 feet (1.5 meters) tall, but its ancestor was another Pleistocene giant, the *Procoptodon*. This was a "mega-roo" that was twice as big as the red kangaroo. *Procoptodons* probably lived like kangaroos do now, in groups and hopping around to feed on grass and bushes.

New Zealand's biggest animals were birds. The moa was a huge, flightless bird that weighed as much as a pony and grew to 9 feet (3 meters) tall. Today, moas are extinct. Humans killed the last of them a few hundred years ago.

The moa laid giant eggs measuring up to 8 in (20 cm) across.

A WARMER WORLD

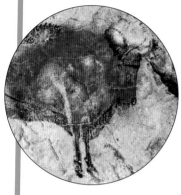

▲ Experts think this cave painting of a bison was made about 20,000 years ago.

The last ice age ended about 10,000 years ago, when most of the great ice sheets melted. Since then, we have been living in warmer times.

When the last ice age ended, life became easier for many animals. However, research shows that the great warm-up was not a slow event—the climate probably changed in less than 100 years. This was too fast for some kinds of animals to adjust. Ice age giants, such as the woolly rhino and almost all mammoths, died out.

Ice age humans probably helped kill off some species, too. Cave paintings show spear-equipped hunters chasing mammoth, deer, and bison.

▲ The Aurochs was a huge ox that had horns up to 13 ft (4 m) across and weighed more than a ton.

▲ Humans were deadly hunters. Even the biggest animal had little defense against a group of humans attacking with sharp spears.

Today, many scientists worry more about Earth getting too hot than about the world plunging into another ice age. Pollution from human activities seems to be slowly raising temperatures on the planet.

Recent studies have shown that the ice cap covering the North Pole is much thinner than it was in 1970. If the world continues warming at its present rate, the ice cap could melt completely by the year 2080, leaving open ocean in its place.

GOOD-BYE ICE CAPS?

Could cold-loving animals survive if the ice melted at Earth's poles? It would be easier for some than for others. Animals such as polar bears would be very badly affected by melting ice. The Arctic ice cap floats on open ocean, so large parts of the polar bear's habitat would turn to water.

Humans would also be badly affected if the ice on Antarctica melted. Sea levels around the world would rise and thousands of coastal towns and cities would be flooded.

ICE AGE BEASTS WORDS

Here are some technical terms used in this book.

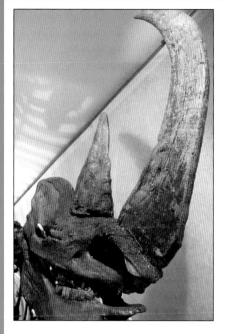

▲ This woolly rhino's skull shows its two huge horns.

Antler
The branched horns of a deer. They fall off in autumn and grow back the following year.

Armor
Thick skin grown by some animals. Glyptodonts in South America had scales that protected them from predators.

Climate
A general word that describes the long-term weather patterns of a place or region.

Continent
One of Earth's main land masses. Africa, Asia, Europe, North and South America, Antarctica, and Australia are Earth's seven continents.

Extinct
An animal or plant species that has died out.

Glacier
A huge mass of ice that moves slowly downhill like a river of ice. Glaciers often make valleys by grinding away rock and soil.

Isthmus
A narrow neck of land that joins two larger areas of land. The Isthmus of Panama joins North and South America.

Land bridge
A shallow part of the ocean floor that becomes dry land if the sea level drops, joining places that were once separated by water. During the Pleistocene, huge amounts of oceanwater were frozen, and sea levels fell hundreds of feet.

Mammal
A warm-blooded animal that gives birth to live young and that feed on its mother's milk.

Marsupial
A type of mammal that has a pouch in which its babies are kept while they feed on their mother's milk. Kangaroos and opossums are marsupials.

Mineral
A nonliving material that occurs naturally in the earth. Many minerals are essential to life. For example, the mineral calcium is needed for bones to grow and be strong.

Pleistocene

The period of time from 1.6 million years ago to 10,000 years ago, during which the Earth was going through its last series of ice ages.

Poles

The coldest parts of Earth, at the north and south ends of the planet. Both poles are covered with ice caps.

Pollution

Harmful waste, such as exhaust fumes from vehicles, released into the environment.

Prey

An animal that is hunted by another animal for food.

Species

A group of living things that can breed among themselves, and have young that can also do the same.

Tar pit

A lake of sticky black liquid, formed when crude oil seeps to the surface through cracks in rocks below ground.

WEIRD WORDS

This pronunciation guide will help you say the ice age words in this book.

Aurochs
or-rox

Casteroides
cass-ter-oy-deez

Coelodonta
see-low-don-ta

Dicrocerus
dik-ross-er-us

Diprotodon
dip-rot-oh-don

Doedicurus
dee-dik-er-us

Elasmotherium
ell-az-moh-theer-ee-um

Glyptodont
glip-toe-dont

Hyena
hi-ee-na

Macrauchenia
mack-raw-keen-ee-uh

Megaloceros
mega-loss-er-oss

Megatherium
mega-theer-ee-um

Panthera leo spelaea
pan-thair-ra lee-oh spel-aye-ah

Pleistocene
ply-stoh-seen

Procoptodon
pro-kop-toe-don

Rhinoceros
rye-noss-er-uss

Siberia
si-beer-ree-ah

Smilodon
smil-oh-don

Thylacinus
thil-ack-in-us

Thylacoleo
thil-ack-oh-lee-oh

Ursus spelaeus
er-sus spel-aye-us

*six-sided scales
(scutes)*

◀ These remains of a glyptodont show its armored body.

ICE AGE BEASTS FACTS

Here are some facts and stories about the ice age world.

Many ice ages

Researchers have evidence of at least 20 ice ages, stretching back millions of years. Ideas to explain them range from wobbles in Earth's path around the Sun to times when we are surrounded by space dust. Events like these reduce the heat Earth receives from the Sun. A drop of just a few degrees is all it takes to plunge Earth into an ice age.

Bridge across the water

Ocean levels fell many feet during the ice ages because ocean water was frozen. Places that had been a seabed became "land bridges" that lasted for thousands of years. For example, Great Britain was once joined to Europe, and North America was joined to Asia. Many animals and people of early human tribes crossed land bridges to new places.

Museum monsters

Dinosaurs are usually more popular than ice age beasts, but it was not always so. In early Victorian times, no dinosaurs had yet been found. Ice age animals were the oldest creatures thought to exist. In fact, most people thought that Earth was just 6,000 years old, instead of the 4.5 billion years that is presently estimated.

Tusk traders

There was once a big trade in mammoth tusks. The ivory was

◄ The prehistoric North American bison was bigger than today's bison, and lived in smaller herds. It also had much longer horns.

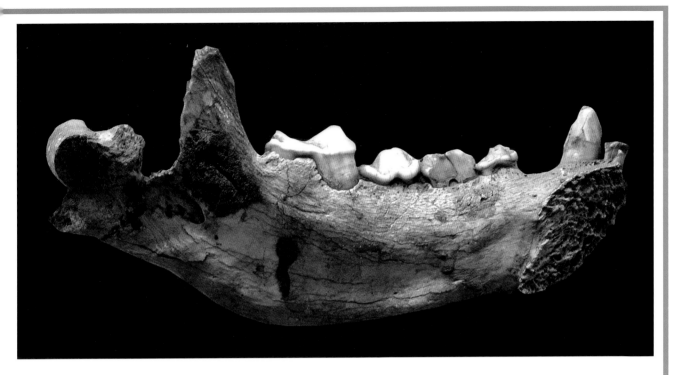

carved into works of art and items such as combs. In the early twentieth century, tusks from more than 200 mammoths (a total weight of about 20 tons) were sold each year in Siberian markets.Mammoth tusks are still valuable—a tusk in good condition can be worth $1,000.

Mammoths as food

From time to time, frozen mammoth remains are found in perfect condition. In the past, people have actually eaten thawed-out mammoth flesh. Today, things are different. Mammoth remains are highly valued for science research—a complete mammoth can be worth $1 million or more.

Elk from Ireland?

The *Megaloceros* is also called the "Irish elk," because remains were first found in an Irish bog. But it was not an elk nor was it only from Ireland. *Megaloceros* was a type of deer that lived all over Europe.

Big baby

A newly born mammoth weighed about 200 lbs (90 kg), and grew to about 9–10 tons when adult. Most human babies weigh only 5–9 lbs (2.5–4 kg) at birth.

Tar pit treasures

▲ This jawbone of a cave bear was found in Europe. Bears used the cave as a safe place for their winter sleep.

The tar pits at La Brea in California have preserved a treasure trove of prehistoric animals, including mammoths, bison, saber-toothed cats, and many others. About 1 million bones have been found so far. Some bones date back 8,000 years, and others are more than 40,000 years old.

ICE AGE BEASTS SUMMARY

From time to time, Earth goes through very cold periods called ice ages. During an ice age, glaciers cover large parts of the planet.

The last ice age was at its coldest 18,000–20,000 years ago, in a time called the Pleistocene. Almost one-third of the land was covered in ice and snow. The best-known ice age beast is the woolly mammoth, which had a thick, hairy coat to keep it warm. Other animals living at this time included woolly rhinos and saber-toothed cats. Many lands in the north were frozen, but South America and Australia were not. Animals that lived there did not need to survive very cold winters. The world has warmed up since the ice age, and many ice age beasts have since died out.

▼ Some museums have displays that show ice age animals. Here a giant sloth's skeleton reaches right up to the roof.

ICE AGE BEASTS ON THE WEB

You can find information about ice age beasts on the Internet. Use a search engine and type in the name of the animal you want to find out about. Here are some good sites to start with:

▼ Here are some screenshots from web sites that show ice age beasts.

http://www.bbc.co.uk/beasts

This site is based on the information presented in the acclaimed TV series *Walking with Beasts*. The huge website is jam-packed with facts and includes details of several ice age animals.

http://www.enchantedlearning.com/subjects/mammals/Iceagemammals.shtml

This site has a wealth of information about ice age mammals like the woolly mammoth, saber-toothed tiger, giant ground sloths, and mastadons.

http://www.nature.ca/notebooks/english/icevan.htm

Most of Canada was buried in ice, and this site shows many of the animals that survived in the chilly conditions of Vancouver Island.

http://www.mammothsite.com

The Mammoth Hot Springs in South Dakota are the focus for this site. It is packed with photos and research information.

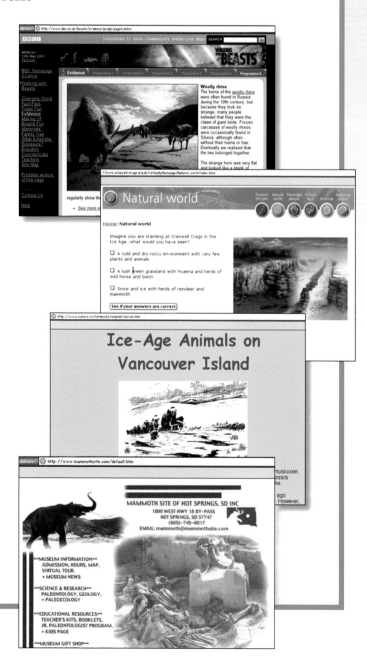

INDEX